My Redeemer Lives

Joyce Savoy (signature)

Messages from the Book of Job
for Lent and Easter

My Redeemer Lives

VERNON R. SCHREIBER

AUGSBURG PUBLISHING HOUSE
Minneapolis, Minnesota

MY REDEEMER LIVES

Copyright © 1974 Augsburg Publishing House

Library of Congress Catalog Card No. 74-14170

International Standard Book No. 0-8066-1453-6

All rights reserved. No part of this book may be used or reproduced in any manner whatsoever without written permission except in the case of brief quotations embodied in critical articles and reviews. For information address Augsburg Publishing House, 426 South Fifth Street, Minneapolis, Minnesota 55415.

Scripture quotations unless otherwise noted are from the Revised Standard Version of the Bible, copyright 1946, 1952, and 1971 by the Division of Christian Education of the National Council of Churches, and are used by permission.

Scripture quotations from the Book of Job are from *Tried and True, Job for Modern Man,* Today's English Version, © 1971 American Bible Society and are used by permission.

Scripture quotations marked TEV are from *Good News for Modern Man,* Today's English Version, © 1966, 1971 American Bible Society.

MANUFACTURED IN THE UNITED STATES OF AMERICA

Contents

About Job and This Book 7

1. He Renews My Faith 9
   Job 1:21

2. He Meets Me Where I Am 17
   Job 9:32-33

3. He Lifts Up the Fallen 26
   Job 16:4-5

4. He Answers Life's Injustices 34
   Job 24:1

5. He Challenges My Righteousness 42
   Job 31:4

6. He Risks Everything 51
   Job 35:6

7. He Bears My Sorrows *(Good Friday)* 59
   Job 30:12

8. He Opens My Eyes *(Easter)* 71
   Job 42:5

About Job and This Book

This series on the Book of Job was first preached at Faith Church, Arlington Heights, Illinois. These messages were first of all a response to the daily trials and disappointments we find ourselves enumerating in our Sunday morning prayers. However, the message of Job concerns itself with a deeper problem than that of momentary emergencies or trials. Whatever their outward circumstances, people today find themselves standing at the edge of an abyss of uncertainty and fear concerning the future. In this respect they share in the predicament which is at the heart of the story of Job. Job's suffering goes beyond physical pain. It includes the agony of wondering whether there is any reason at all for hoping in God.

This sense of bewilderment makes Job's struggle the struggle of every man. It is a struggle which also leads us to look beyond Job to the form of another man of sorrows, Jesus of Nazareth. It is in and through Jesus, the suffering servant of the Lord, that we can begin to perceive the outline of God's love against a darkened sky. Stirred by Job's questions about the meaning of life under an apparently silent God, we are equipped with a new sensitivity towards the essential message of the Lenten season and its portrayal of the Son of God lifted up on a cross.

My preparation for this series convinced me that the Book of Job deserved attention and reflection that would go beyond weekly sermons. Therefore, with the sermon at the heart of a given section of Job, additional notes for the daily study of each chapter of Job were prepared for distribution. These meditations are available in a separate devotional booklet, *My Servant Job*, and may be used for personal or family reading. Throughout these devotions I have used the American Bible Society's translation of Job, the complete text of which is contained in *My Servant Job*. In my estimation, this translation does more than any other to provide the reader with a readily understandable version of the entire Book of Job.

The sermons take up the theme of what should be our response to the trials of life. They also lead us into questions concerning our relationship with God. Can I hope in God? Why has this happened to me? What judgment should I make about the suffering of others? Is God just? They also help us to explore the great themes in the Book of Job related to the ethical life, God's ways with man, and the meaning of a living faith.

1.

> The Lord gave, and now he has taken away. May his name be praised! (Job 1:21).

He Renews My Faith

On this Ash Wednesday imagine that you have the power to look down the corridors of history into ancient biblical times. You see a grove of olive trees near the brook Kidron. You see a man in that garden. It is obvious that a great burden of suffering is weighing him down, but it is also evident that he is in an act of prayer to the Father in heaven whom he continues to trust. His name is Jesus.

Then you look beyond that garden and see the more distant figure of another man who lies prostrate on sandy soil near a nomad's camp. The time is many centuries before the time of Jesus. But this man also shows the weight of great sorrow. He, too, is praying, and in that prayer he is praising the God in whom he trusts. His name is Job.

Jesus and Job. Both these men are mighty figures who lead us into a search for the meaning of suffering and our response to such suffering. Because we are entering into a study of the Book of Job, we will look first of all towards the more distant and less familiar of the two figures, the man called Job.

As we see him there on the ground, a great wave of tragedy has just swept over his life. First a servant had rushed in to tell him that he had lost all his property. One bearer of bad news follows after the other until at last comes the worst news of all. Job's children had all gathered at the home of his eldest son. But while they were in the midst of a festive celebration a sudden storm, much like one of those "twisters" which suddenly form on the plains of the Midwest, had swept down on the house. When it had passed, not one son or daughter was left alive. Reeling under the shock of this news, Job has withdrawn from the others, shaved his head as a sign of his great sorrow, and hurled himself upon the ground. But now, in the midst of such grief, this early "man of sorrows" lifts up his head and offers up a great cry of faith, "The Lord gave, and now he has taken away. May his name be praised!"

Why had this great trouble befallen Job? We will find many answers to this question as we study his life. Some of the answers, however, seem only to raise further questions. For instance, the beginning of the Book of Job raises its own set of questions. It begins with a picture of God and Satan engaged in a sort of summit meeting. The puzzling aspect of this meeting can be understood by imagining a summit meeting between two great powers, such as the United States and China. Such meetings do take place, of course; but imagine one or the other of the two leaders agreeing, simply for the sake of proving how loyal his countrymen are, to an agreement which puts his

He Renews My Faith

own people under the thumb of the other. Yet it is in such terms that God is pictured as agreeing to permit Job to endure great trials and testings.

It is for this reason that some have questioned whether such a summit meeting actually took place in the chambers of heaven. They point out that since the Book of Job is clearly cast in the form of a drama, this opening scene as it is written may simply be a dramatic method for framing the basic problem being dealt with in this book. Others believe that it happened just this way.

Whichever interpretation you choose, the real question, however, remains the same. That question goes beyond the nature of that opening summit meeting. The great question of the Book of Job and of life itself is simply this: can a man remain faithful to God when it seems that God has deserted him in the midst of his troubles and left him alone and unattended? For the fact remains that when trouble comes we are always hard put to understand it and to accept it. Despite all our explanations, there is always an element of mystery attached to the way trouble seems to come in such a large measure to certain families. There is always an element of surprise and bewilderment when trouble strikes our own lives, whether that suffering takes the form of a sudden heart attack, or the loss of one's job, or some other cloud which blots out what we thought was going to be a bright and sunny future.

Pride Prevents Praise

We shall not find our answer by simply saying that our troubles are probably insignificant compared to those of Job. Perhaps they are, but the point is that no trouble is insignificant if it is being used by Satan as a device by which he is leading us to stop praising and serving God. Therefore, as we enter into a mood of heightened self-examination which is to be a characteristic of the Lenten season, we would do well to ask ourselves not only what "bad" deeds we have been engaged in but also what has happened to our habit of praising God at all times. For the pride of the human heart finds all kinds of reasons for not giving him the praise that is his due. When times are good, we forget that God is the giver of all good things and become religious "Little Jack Horners" about whom the nursery rhyme says, "He stuck in his thumb, pulled out a plum, and said, 'What a good boy am I!'" This same spirit of pride makes it easy to say, when things are going badly, "Why should I praise God when unfair things such as this are happening to me?" Let's face it: we find it easy to boast, easy to complain, but not to give praise.

Trouble as the Anvil of God

However, trouble can lead to one other response, and that is what Job teaches us in this opening chapter. Trouble can be a means by which we are kept from drifting from God. The Hebrew mind—and this mind was shaped by the revelation God made of himself throughout the Old Testament—could not conceive of anything happening apart from the will of the Lord; but when it saw the hand of the Lord, it saw God's love as well. We, too, can discover trouble as the anvil of God on which his Word strikes down in such a way as to awaken our sleepy hearts. In times of trouble we can hear the voice of God saying to us, "No, I will not let you go your own way, a way that will lead to your destruction. I will not let you think that you have it made all on your own. In the midst of this trouble, I, the Lord your God, want you for the sake of your own safety, to ask with a new awareness, 'Whose man or woman am I, God's or Satan's?' "

The writer of the Letter to the Hebrews makes this point as he quotes from the Old Testament Book of Proverbs: " 'My son, do not regard lightly the discipline of the Lord, nor lose courage when you are punished by him. For the Lord disciplines him whom he loves, and chastises every son whom he receives.' It is for discipline that you have to endure. God is treating you as sons; for what son is there whom his father does not discipline?" (Hebrews 12:5-7).

The Praise of God for His Own Sake

Does this explanation of trouble seem to be too easy and quick? We do not intend it to serve that purpose. On the contrary, that is why we are entering into an in-depth study of the Book of Job. We want to explore fully the questions that arise when trouble strikes hard. But the fact that there are still many questions to be asked does not change the importance of what Job is able to say in this first chapter. From the beginning we can find in the story of Job a picture of what life is like for us as well. As we examine ourselves, we may see that we, like Job, need to fight our way back to a hold on God which is in danger of slipping. We, too, may need to come up out of the fire of bereavement and loss, not cursing God as Job's wife was soon to suggest, but praising God for his own sake. What a great statement this is: "The Lord gave and now he has taken away. May his name be praised!" In order to praise God in this manner, simply because he is God, a man must be sure of God; and at this point, Job was.

But what about you? Do you have what it takes to praise God simply for what he is, whatever your own personal circumstances might be? It is through this question that God would lead you to find the answer in the one place it can be found, the person of Christ. To praise God for his own sake, you must be sure of God. To be sure of God you must know God. To know God you must know Christ Jesus. He is the full revelation of God. He is the final evidence that no matter what may happen, you *are* loved by God.

To receive the full picture of that evidence, we now think back to that other figure kneeling in the act of prayer. We look now at Jesus in the Garden of Gethsemane. His burden is heavy. He knows that the time is at hand for his betrayal, arrest, trial and bloody death upon the Cross. As he prays he asks his Father if there is not a way out. "Nevertheless," he continues, "not my will but thine be done." This is another way of saying, "Father, you have given me my life. Now you may take away that life, but you are still Number One with me. I want what you want. May your name be praised!"

If only we could see, once and for all, that God is speaking directly to us through the life of Jesus!

Have we dared to imagine that for some reason God has turned his back on his children and that his will and purpose for us is less than good and perfect? Has not our complaining spirit suggested that this is what we are really thinking even if we would not admit it in so many words?

In answer to this unfounded spirit of resentment God offers us this compelling scene of Jesus in the Garden of Gethsemane. It is an answer that goes far beyond presenting us with an example of how we *ought* to behave. Our heavenly Father is reassuring us that in his love he has sent his Son to take up every burden that we might be called upon to bear. Are we confronted by sorrow, injustice, death? So was our Lord. The prophet Isaiah has captured the picture when he writes, "Surely he has borne our griefs and carried our sorrows . . . . He was wounded for our transgressions, he was bruised for our iniquities; upon him was the chastisement that made us whole" (Isaiah 53:4-5).

Stepping Out on the High Road of Praise

Would you praise God at all times and in all places? It will be the experience of God's unmerited and overwhelming love in Christ that will open your mouth and let loose those words. Praise cannot be faked. It must rise out of an unshakable confidence in the unchanging love of God. It provides the witness that this anxious and unhappy world is looking for. An unsung example of such a witness was given one night by a black woman, a poor woman, who was telling a dinner companion of the struggle she and her husband endured as they sought to feed nine children and keep the older ones working hard at their studies in high school. As if this were not enough, their third son had suffered brain damage. One day he would be alert and receptive, the next day no one could get through to him. They were waiting for the opening of a special children's center in the ghetto where they lived. "But I don't complain," she said. "And I don't get impatient with God. What he is going to do he is going to do. So I just stay in there." Though she did not add the words, her face clearly said, "And may his name be praised!"

To speak in such a manner, you must be sure of God. To be sure of God you must know God. So let this be our first step in this new Lenten season and in our study of the struggle of Job. In your own heart tell God that you want to know him better by learning in greater depth the love Jesus Christ has for you. It is in him that our victory begins. It is in him that we find the strength and joy to show that we mean it when we say, "May his name be praised!"

2.

If God were human I could answer him back; we could go to court to decide our quarrel. But there is no one to step between us—no one to judge both God and me (Job 9:32-33; cp. Job 3:1-10:22).

He Meets Me Where I Am

In the season of Lent as in perhaps no other season of the year we are aware that the people of the Bible are not cardboard figures who bear little resemblance to the flesh-and-blood people we live with day by day. They possess the full range of human weaknesses and human emotions. We think of the fickle crowds who so eagerly greeted Jesus and were then just as quickly turned away from their initial enthusiasm. We think of the disciples whose resolution and professed loyalty vanished from sight at the first sign of stress. Job also shows the same human frailties common to us all. Our first glimpse of the man showed him in a moment of triumphant faith. He had withstood the sudden loss of his wealth and his children without losing his faith in God. We, too, often will meet a sudden crisis with a strength which surprises even ourselves. But wars are not won after one battle, and Job found this out. A terrible, disgusting, unchanging disease became his lot, and it seemed that there would be no turning in this pathway of suffering. It is this long-term trouble that keeps on grinding away at the very core of our spirit which puts our human resources to their severest test. In that kind of crisis we discover how many deep and distressing emotions can attack our faith.

Shock

Students of human behavior have observed that there is a general pattern of response to the kind of trial and trouble we are talking about. There may be variations in this pattern, of course; but there is a basically typical pattern. The first stage is one of shock. People cannot believe that what has happened to them has really happened. Perhaps it is the diagnosis that you have a terminal illness, or that your job is gone, or that a child has gone completely off the deep end. There is a feeling that it just cannot be and that, "like a bad dream," it will all go away on the morrow.

Anger

The next stage of response is one in which there is the feeling of anger. As we work our way into the Book of Job, we find, after an initially beautiful statement of faith and silent suffering, that Job suddenly bursts out with an unchecked statement of anger. He is angry about what has happened, and he makes no bones about it. "God, put a curse on the day I was born; put a curse on the night when I was conceived" (3:2-3).

We must not be afraid to own up to our feelings

of anger. On one occasion a pastor confessed from the pulpit his great feelings of anger over what seemed to be the senseless waste of a marvelous young Christian mother who was a member of the congregation. Slowly but surely she had been ravaged by a malignant tumor of the brain. The pastor had come back from the visitation hour at the funeral parlor and shouted his anger both to and at a God whom he knew was nevertheless listening to his protest over what seemed to be such a waste. It was only after he had vented this honest anger that he could compose what was also the message of hope that God still gives even in our darkest hour of despair and incomprehension.

Perhaps some would say that a pastor should not confess such feelings and that people expect better things from him. But the result of this confession was an act of cleansing he had not expected. The next day he received an anonymous letter. The woman who wrote the letter thanked him for speaking as he had because she had had just such feelings about the suffering and death of her Christian mother but had not felt free until then to share those feelings of anger with anyone else because she had been taught that such feelings were so terribly wrong. She had tried to make herself less than human. The only consequence had been that she carried not only her anger but a feeling of guilt as well. Now she was talking about it and finding a new freedom.

We should never try to deny the existence of anger as a common form of response to the troubles that come upon us. Like tears, anger is often a way of expressing one's heartache, and the angry person you know is often simply a person who feels deeply and terribly wounded. Rather than refusing to admit the existence of such feelings, anger must often be honestly expressed before genuine reconciliation can take place. The denial of anger is not what is needed, but rather the recognition that to *continue* in a condition of anger, loaded down with self-pity and resentment, is the path to self-destruction. While we do not deny anger, we also know that we must go beyond it.

Appeasement

How do we go beyond anger? In Job's case his friends told him that he should stop being angry and instead make amends to God, for surely he must have sinned against God in some terrible way. Otherwise all this would not be happening to him! There is a very strong instinct at work in this frequently heard advice. It is the instinct that religion can be defined on the basis of deeds being followed by appropriate rewards. If you have been good, good will follow. If you have been bad, bad will follow. If bad things have been happening, then it is up to you to set things right with God so that good things can start coming your way again. Job's friend named Eliphaz puts it bluntly, "Think back now. Name a single case when a righteous man met with disaster" (4:7). He is implying in no uncertain terms that Job had these sufferings coming to him. He continues, "Can a man be right in the sight of God? Can anyone be pure before his Creator?" (4:17). He also declares, "Man brings trouble on himself, as surely as sparks fly up from a fire" (5:7). There seems to be a great deal of truth in what he is saying. What then is wrong? What is wrong is that Eliphaz would throw the entire burden of responsibility upon the sufferer, making him think that somehow he must show the right spirit and that then he will be able to get out from under his trouble? But this demand to "set things right" results only in greater frustration and doubt on the part of the sufferer.

Depression

Job refuses to consider for a moment this kind of appeasement. Instead he plunges directly from anger into depression, another stage of feeling which is typically a part of the pattern of human behavior. A letter from a woman suffering from an increasingly crippling disease shows how even the faithful can find themselves caught up in such a state of depression. She had both prayed about and fought against this growing disability. She writes, "I know I'm no better than anyone else, but I was so happy before my legs went on me. First I thought that maybe my faith was being tested. Then maybe that God had other plans for me." We can well imagine how this believing child of God carefully examined her faith in God whom she worshiped and loved. Then she continues, "But now I don't know. I seem to be falling away from everything and everyone." Yes, depression will come.

What do you tell someone who is experiencing some grinding, unrelenting trouble which only seems to mount in its severity? Do you teach them a theology of retribution which says that God is just and that therefore you must be paying for *something*, something you will not confess or perhaps have forgotten? What a cruel religion that is! It is against this twisting of the truth that Job is fighting when he tells them that all he wants from them is a little understanding. We must admit that Job had his own problem of pride. On the other hand, it helped not at all that when he cries out for a little understanding, Bildad's only response is to say that not only is Job a stubborn sinner but that he is a windbag as well (8:1). All kinds of feelings have been expressed: anger, appeasement, depression, but no one is getting anywhere!

A Wonderful Mediator

What we are witnessing in the advice of Job's friends is the outlook of man when he has no religion or only a religion of his own devising and understanding. When we hear Job's lament, "If God were human, I could answer him back. We could go to court and decide our quarrel. But there is no one to step between us—no one to judge both God and me" (9:32-33), we are hearing the cry of someone who still has not had the privilege of seeing the full revelation of God's way through his Son, Jesus. If God were human, we could have this out! But God has become human. He has come in the person of Jesus of Nazareth. Jesus has come with the glory of the Father within him, and yet as "a man of sorrows and acquainted with grief" (Isaiah 53:3).

Job, in the name of all the tormented and troubled,

He Meets Me Where I Am

has shouted, "God, come into court with me! We have a few things to straighten out." God comes; he comes in the person of Jesus.

"Look at my sores!" Job cries.

"Look at the crown of thorns piercing my scalp, and see the open wound in my side," Jesus replies.

"My bones ache to their very marrow," Job laments.

Jesus says, "See my hands and feet pierced by these rusty nails."

"I am tormented!" Job cries.

"I thirst!" comes the reply.

Job complains, "The spitefulness of my so-called friends!"

Jesus says, "They forsook me, too, and fled."

Job says bitterly, "Eliphaz says that I am judged by God."

Jesus recalls, "The crowds about me called out, 'He trusted in God. Let God deliver him now.' They considered me to be smitten and stricken by God as a terrible sinner."

"Bildad called me a windbag!"

"Peter denied me with a curse."

"Zophar was willing to hand me over to the punishment of God without a word of comfort."

"Judas sold me for thirty pieces of silver."

We may come before the bar of justice all bedraggled and beaten, wanting to have it out with God; but we find someone else in the courtroom who has suffered and bled much more than we. We look closely at this broken piece of humanity and discover that we are seeing him in whom dwells "the fullness of the Godhead bodily" (Colossians 2:9). How strange and marvelous is our God! On the one hand he is all might and power. Then he becomes a worm, someone of no account at all. In this condition he steps out before us and tells us that he has suffered everything on our behalf, and that through his suffering God has reconciled us to himself if only we will accept his love. Yes, trying and difficult events come our way, and we dare not deny the feelings which pass through our hearts and minds. But then from his own cross God tells you to take your pride, your anger, your efforts at appeasement, and your depression and let them all be swallowed up in his love for you, a love revealed in the "one mediator between God and men, the man Christ Jesus" (Timothy 2:5). In the midst of our trials Christ stands as the sign of God that the hand of his wrath has been lifted. Will you turn your back and not give this wonderfully strange God scarcely another thought, or will you give him your heart as he asks?

But what if trouble continues on and on? If so, can all this talk about a Mediator making peace really be true? One of the problems of Job's well-intentioned friends was that they felt that they had to provide a complete answer for everything. It is a trap preachers can fall into, too. There are situations where the human tongue must be silent because only God can give the answer as he speaks to the human heart still willing to trust him. As a concluding example, there was a Christian who endured great physical distress but was filled with the Spirit and the gift of great faith. Consequently there were great hopes for recovery and renewed life. Instead there was a continued wasting and weakening which finally resulted in death.

"Well, he lost anyway," some might say. "He lost." But those who watched him die and heard his last prayer would reply, "No, he won!" That's the promise given to us, too. When we go to court, whom do we find? We find a friend! Jesus!

3.   If you were in my place and I in yours, I could say everything you are saying. I could shake my head wisely and drown you in a flood of words (Job 16:4-5).

He Lifts Up the Fallen

About the third week in Lent you are apt to hear the remark, "Lent certainly isn't what it used to be." Or, "What has happened to our Sunday church attendance?" Or, "People just don't seem to have the same commitment any more." Since Lent is a season when we are talking much about renewing a spirit of repentance and faith, this is a most appropriate time to ask about those who apparently have given up on the faith, on Bible reading, and on most of the specific content of Christian teachings. Some of them, as Jesus teaches in the Parable of the Sower and the Seed, have been choked off by the "cares and pleasures and riches of life" (Luke 8:14). Others, however, may have lost hope in God. They have given up in the face of the troubles of this world, either their own or the sufferings they see among others. "Where is God?" they ask. "Why doesn't God do something to straighten things out?" Like Job, they are bitter and disheartened; and there is no one to help restore their faith.

The friends of Job—Eliphaz, Bildad, and Zophar—thought that they were helping to restore Job, but they had two terrible faults which destroyed their effectiveness. In both cases their trouble was that there simply was no love at all coming through.

A Theology of Retribution

Their first fault was that they had a theology of retribution. They had the simplistic belief that here on earth God will always bless the good and punish the evil, and that if you were suffering greatly it meant that you had sinned greatly. Since Job was suffering greatly, it must be that he had secretly committed some heinous sin which demanded this kind of suffering. Unfortunately, the same kind of theology often prevails among church members today. If trouble befalls someone, there are people who will think, "Well, it probably serves him right. I always have had the idea that he is not nearly as good as he makes out to be." It is a terrible thing when such a spirit arises among people so that others are judged as sinners because of the calamities that have come upon them. What they—Job's friends and people today—fail to see is that if God's love comes only when it is deserved, then it is not love any more.

An Attitude of Self-righteousness

There is an attitude which inevitably accompanies this kind of tit-for-tat theology. It is the attitude of self-righteousness. For in judging others as those who are suffering for their sins you are saying that you yourself are righteous. When this spirit of self-righteousness comes through, the chances of anyone being restored to faith are just about nil, no matter how eloquent the words. That is what is wrong with the message of Zophar, although the words themselves sound so correct and right: "Put your heart right, Job. Reach out to God. Put away evil and wrong from your home. Then face the world again, firm and courageous. Then all your troubles will fade from your memory, like floods that are past and remembered no more" (11:13-16). When Eliphaz continues in the same vein, his added air of superiority only serves to increase the feeling of resentment on the part of Job who cries out, "If you were in my place and I in yours, I could say everything you are saying. I could shake my head wisely and drown you in a flood of words" (16:4). Nothing turns away a person who is experiencing doubt and despair more than the refusal of someone else to listen to their appeal to "walk where I have walked." The spirit of self-righteousness is one of the greatest obstacles to the restoration of the fallen. It was present in some of the Pharisees who had nothing but contempt for the sinners whom Jesus loved. It is present in us. In this matter we must confess that we have not only been sinned against but have sinned against others.

Driven to God Alone

We should be careful, however, not to give the impression that we think Job deserves to be excused as he keeps arguing that he is completely innocent and deserves none of these things which have happened

He Lifts Up the Fallen

to him. The lack of genuine comfort on the part of his friends has led him to become, again and again, just as self-righteous as they. Forced into a position of defensiveness, it often seems that he is basing his entire hope on his own innocence, and that only makes matters worse for him.

At other moments, however, this lack of true communication with his friends (for communication always includes listening as well as talking) leads Job to reach out to God as his only source of hope. Condemned but never comforted, Job describes his appalling physical condition: "My wife can't stand the smell of my breath, and my own brothers won't come near me. My skin hangs loose on my bones" (19:17, 20). Then, in the very midst of these words describing his terrible anguish, Job utters the words most familiarly known to us in the translation: "I know that my Redeemer lives, and at last he will stand upon the earth; and after my skin has been thus destroyed, then from my flesh I shall see God; whom I shall see on my side, and my eyes behold, and not another" (19:25-27 RSV). Or as Today's English Version puts it, "But I know there is someone in heaven who will come at last to my defense." It is difficult to explain the majesty of these words except as a moment of the Holy Spirit. Crushed by woe, judged by his peers, a man is led to reach out to a redeeming God with a hope that passes human understanding.

This great affirmation points us to the way of restoration for every sinner, beginning with ourselves. In God's Word the explanation of life goes far beyond theories of judgment or retribution. Restoration of faith comes through the God-given insight that there is a Redeemer who stands by our side, and that through him the victory shall come at last. What Job was able to say from his Old Testament vantage point we can also repeat today: "I know that my Redeemer lives." He is Jesus Christ, the righteous one who died for my sins.

Does the charge come against you that you have sinned and deserve punishment? Let the charge be repeated, Martin Luther once wrote, for therein lies your consolation. The proclamation of the New Testament is not a message of retribution, but good news about the rescue of the sinner through Jesus Christ the righteous one.

"You're not so good," someone says. "You've got plenty of sins that deserve to be paid for."

"Thank you for your consolation," you can reply, "for as hard as I find it to remember sometimes, Christ was given on the Cross not for the holy, the righteous and the deserving, but for sinners, for those who were his enemies, for the godless, for the undeserving of anything but eternal death. How good of you to remind me that I am a sinner."

"But then you will be punished on earth through much suffering and damned in hell," the accuser will say.

"No," you answer, "for I take my refuge in Christ. He died for sinners. That's why I thank you for reminding me that I am a sinner. When you call me a sinner you are preaching the glory of God to me, for you are reminding me, a miserable and condemned sinner, of the fatherly love of God. You are reminding me of him who 'so loved the world that he gave his

He Lifts Up the Fallen 31

only-begotten Son' (John 3:16). You are reminding me of the prophet Isaiah's assurance that 'the Lord laid on him the iniquity of us all,' and that 'for the transgressions of his people he was stricken" (Isaiah 53:6,8)."

Shout your thanks to heaven that you have been reminded that you are sinner, for that puts you back on the track that leads to real restoration.

A New Spirit Towards Others

This consolation, born of the love of God for sinners, will create a new spirit in us towards others. It will develop an attitude which will more effectively work for the restoration of those who have drifted off from God because the pressures and troubles of this world have been just too much for them.

A powerful example for us to follow lies in the very heart of the Passion Story. Jesus and his disciples are gathered in the Upper Room. They are there to celebrate the Passover, but there is much more gloom than joy. The disciples have even argued amongst themselves. Tension fills the air. Then with loving eyes Jesus looks at the man called Peter. "Simon, Simon, behold, Satan demanded to have you, that he might sift you like wheat." How reminiscent these words of Satan's claim on Job's life made in the first chapter of the Book of Job! Then Jesus continues, "But I have prayed for you that your faith may not fail; and when you have turned again, strengthen your brethren" (Luke 22:31-32). Despite the bombastic disciple's protest that he is ready to go to prison and to death with Jesus, the Lord has seen an inner flaw in Peter. But he also sees beneath that flaw to the new man God's Spirit will create. Seeing that restoration which will take place by the power of God, Jesus then calls on Peter to strengthen and restore others as well.

Has someone drifted away from God, perhaps in a state of great bitterness and disillusionment? That person is indeed a sinner—just like you and me. But this is no time to take on an air of superiority. How can there be such an attitude when the only truly righteous people in the sight of God are "deserters" who have been restored by Christ's death? That is why we ought to cringe at the indifferent dismissal uttered by people inside the church concerning those who have drifted away: "It's time we cleared out all the dead wood." It is true that we should seek to be honest and clear-eyed about who is really with the Lord and who is not, but we are not talking about *wood*! We are talking about people. We are talking about people with the potential of complete restoration when the hope of the Redeemer is made alive to them once again. This awareness of the potential victory of God also lies behind the Apostle Paul's admonition to the Galatians, "Brethren, if a man is overtaken in any trespass, you who are spiritual should restore him in a spirit of gentleness. Look to yourself, lest you too be tempted" (Galatians 6:1).

Restoration comes, not through judgment, not through an air of superiority, not through teaching a theology of retribution, but through a spirit of gentleness leading a person to see the sacrificial love of Christ. Restoration, not retribution, that is where our joy should be found. But to so restore one another, we must be restored ourselves. Do you know that your Redeemer lives and what kind of Redeemer he has been for you? When a sinner gives an emphatic "Yes!" to that question his restoration begins.

4.

Why doesn't God set a time for judging, a day of justice for those who serve him? (Job 24:1).

He Answers Life's Injustices

A respected polling organization took a poll in one of our largest states to determine how much people "trusted" public figures. It turned out that only two of six men could garner the votes of a slight majority. The people's mayor was trusted the least, and the governor of their state was the next lowest on their credibility scale. A news commentator ranked the highest; and right in the middle, only two percentage points lower than the nation's president, stood "David Levy," not a real person but simply an extra name inserted into the questionnaire. Perhaps these results do not surprise us, but the results of the poll bring us a sobering lesson: people do not trust those in power, considering them to be out for themselves, either for more power, or status, or money. Who can say that there is overwhelming evidence that they should think otherwise?

It would also seem likely that these people who were polled were expressing a general attitude of dis-

He Answers Life's Injustices

trust towards an entire society, a society which is "on the make." Perhaps in their own secret thoughts they would even admit to themselves that they would do the same if they had the chance. For this truly seems to be a society in which people with the right connections can do or exhibit almost anything they want and, with few exceptions, end up with a fat bank account and no trouble at all.

Is such an attitude overly cynical? Not many businessmen or politicians would argue the point. Certainly Job, the giant figure from the Old Testament whose trials we have been studying, would not have objected. For he expressed exactly these feelings about the ascendancy of injustice over justice as he spoke to his friends in answer to their argument that suffering is always the consequence of man's sin. He asks,

> Why does God let evil men grow old and prosper?
> Their children and grandchildren grow up before
>   their very eyes.
> God does not bring disaster on their homes;
>   they never have to live in terror.
> Yes, all their cattle breed and give birth without
>   trouble.
> Their children run and play like lambs
>   and dance to the music of harps and flutes.
> They live out their lives in peace,
>   and die quietly without suffering (21:7-13).

Job asks his accusers,

> Haven't you talked with people who travel?
> Don't you know the reports they bring back?
> On the day when God is angry and punishes,
>   it is the wicked man who is always spared.

> There is no one to accuse a wicked man,
>   or pay him back for all he has done.
> When he is carried to the graveyard,
>   to where his tomb is guarded,
> thousands join the funeral procession,
>   and even the earth lies gently on his body
>   (21:29-33).

Shades of the gangster funerals of our own day! When Job speaks about the mockery of justice, we think we are reading the headlines about today's scandals:

> Men move boundary markers to get more land;
>   they steal sheep and put them with their own flocks.
> They steal donkeys that belong to orphans,
>   and keep a widow's ox till she pays her debts.
> They keep the poor from getting their rights
>   and force the needy to run and hide (24:2-4).

Job does not want to philosophize. He wants to talk about what is really happening: "In the city you hear the cries of the wounded and the dying, but God ignores their prayers" (24:12).

Job lived in "the land of Uz." Insert the names of any major city, any Indian reservation, any town, whether it is in an affluent or deprived section of the country, and it would make no difference concerning the things he has said. There are thousands, yes, millions, who could, if we would offer them pious platitudes about the rewards of virtue, take our words and throw them back in our faces, demanding with one voice that we listen to Job. They may be no better than average, but they also know that the cause for their suffering and oppression is not to be laid at their door. It is the fault of a society in which the practitioners of gross injustice always seem to escape They would say that Job is telling it like it is! The wicked escape.

The wicked escape. Let's carry that point one step further. This also seems to be the point in the story of Jesus' suffering. Consider Barabbas. He sits in his cell, chained to the wall. He has been justly condemned to die. He awaits his last hour. The door opens with a noisy clang. The guard stands over him. Now he will be dragged out to a sadistic execution. There was nothing cool, methodical, or antiseptic about death on a cross compared to modern executions. But wait! His fetters are being struck off. He suddenly finds himself blinking in the sunlight. They tell him that Pilate had offered a choice between Barabbas and Jesus, and that the crowd called for his release. His friends who had been mingling in the crowd tell him that Pilate had asked about Jesus, "Why, what evil has he done?" but then quickly caved in under the pressure of the crowd. Barabbas has escaped and an innocent man suffers instead. Why? Because those in power, the chief priests on the one hand and Pilate on the other, were all more interested in maintaining the status quo for their own advantage than they were in seeing justice done.

The wicked man goes free. Jesus dies. The vaunted righteousness of God is nowhere to be found—until we remember that it was in Christ himself that the mysterious yet divine righteousness of God was at work in our behalf. For through his cross the completely innocent Christ has endured the punishment for sin which should be endured by every one of us. The Apostle Peter, in his own straightforward way which does not try to conceal his own need as a sinner, asserts: "He bore our sins in his body on the tree" (1 Peter 2:24). Paul takes up the same theme about the function and role of the "tree of the cross" in the letter to the Galatians: "Christ redeemed us from the curse of the law, having become a curse for us—for it is written, 'Cursed be every one who hangs on a tree'" (3:13). Martin Luther, in looking at this last piece of Scripture, commented, "Just as Christ is wrapped up in our flesh and blood, so we must . . . know him to be wrapped up in our sins, our curse, our death, and everything evil" (*Luther's Works*, American Edition, Vol. 26, p. 279).

We do not claim that we will ever be able to fully comprehend how this is possible, but Christ died in your place and mine. Put your faith in him. Make him your hope. It is promised that you, the sinner, with no worthwhile or sufficient righteousness of your own, can nevertheless by faith in Christ be counted as righteous in God's sight. The death of Jesus made possible not only the escape of Barabbas. In his death Jesus made possible the escape of the whole world from the consequences of sin. He makes possible *your* escape.

But how does this message about the justice of God at work in Christ relate to the problem we started with: the escape of the wicked and the frightening breakdown of integrity at the very heart of our society? In seeking an answer there are two false leads which can be easily followed. One of them

He Answers Life's Injustices

makes a false use of the very message of the cross which should be a power for change. Like so many "heresies," it has emerged out of a seed of truth which has been twisted or overemphasized. In this case people willingly accept the proposition that the wicked escape, and then continue their reasoning along these lines: "Naturally the wicked escape. But the important thing is to remember that we are *all* wicked and therefore the message we are to proclaim is that all people in this world are sinners and need salvation as Christ provides it. As far as the social order is concerned, it is sick and evil and always will be. But that is not our problem. The church's business is saving souls, not meddling in politics or other matters it knows nothing about." In this line of thinking the cry of Job concerning injustice in the world is not so much denied as it is simply ignored.

On the other end of the scale, there are those who have responded to Job's appeal by deciding that the only meaningful form of religion is one in which you relentlessly seek to set straight everything that is wrong in the world. They have decided that to be religious is to be involved in social action, and that to be involved in social action is to be religious. Furthermore, since they have enlisted God on their side, they are certain that he has made them instant experts and that their proposed solutions are the answers of the Almighty himself. They dismiss proclamation of the Word and worship by the faithful as irrelevant.

What is the answer in these troubled times when injustice and graft have crushed the hopes of so many people? The cross cannot be discarded without changing the very nature of the New Testament's message. We need it. However, we must also recognize that when Peter spoke of how Christ "bore our sins in his body," he went on to make the application that what happened through that "tree" took place so that we might "die to sin and live *for* righteousness" (1 Peter 2:24 TEV). In other words, the good news of Christ is not to be used like a set of blinders so that we do not notice what is really happening in the world. We are not delivered to a never-never land in which we do not have to listen to the appeals of fellow human beings for relief from oppression or deprivation. Hand in hand with the proclamation of the death of Christ on behalf of the wicked, the church must carry out its function in respect to society to speak out against injustice. If our society is gaining an X-rating in the sight of God and man, it needs to be told that this is so. How can it be otherwise? If we are to speak about bearing the cross of our Lord, then we cannot choose to be silent when we ought to speak out. How can we *not* be involved on behalf of justice and righteousness when we have experienced the justice and righteousness of God in the most profound way possible—through his love in Christ?

For Christians it is not a question of how far they will get in standing up to a society where so many are simply out to get what they can for themselves, but a question of which way they will go as they show to others that they have been redeemed so that they might live for righteousness. The unjust and the oppressors may seem to be getting away with their actions right up till judgment day, but that is not what determines our course of action as Christians. When we who are escapees ourselves hear a modern-day Job call for a "day of justice for those who serve (God)" for us, that day is now.

5.

God knows everything I do; he sees every step I take (Job 31:4).

He Challenges My Righteousness

In our study of the Gospel accounts of Jesus' last days before his Crucifixion we tend to become onlookers at the triumphal entrance of Jesus on Palm Sunday and then skip to that night a few days later when Jesus' personal anguish rose to its very climax. But what of the days between? These were not days when Jesus languished in mournful solitude, knowing that his own words, "Behold, we are going up to Jerusalem; and the Son of man will be delivered to the chief priests and scribes, and they will condemn him to death, and deliver him to the Gentiles to be mocked and scourged and crucified" would soon be fulfilled (Matthew 20:18-19).

On the contrary, those days were some of the most productive in terms of his teachings to others. Nor was his instruction merely focused on proper attitudes toward suffering. No, a look at the Gospel according to Matthew shows us that he went daily to the Temple during what we call "Holy Week" and there he taught men how to *live*. He talked about:

He Challenges My Righteousness

faith, prayer, and true obedience;
outreach to the spiritually neglected;
that faithfulness to God which does not deny but on the other hand goes far beyond mere obedience to Caesar;
the hope of the resurrection;
love for your neighbor and true humility;
the making of oaths;
living mercifully and hearing the messengers of God;
signs of the End and of the return of the Son of Man;
proper stewardship and a life of vigilance;
wise use of one's talents; and
the care of the "least of these my brethren" through feeding the hungry, giving a cup of cold water to the thirsty, welcoming the stranger, visiting those who are sick and in prison.

Quite a list! Jesus may have been approaching a time of great personal suffering, but he talked about living. This fact should not be omitted from any study of the Passion history. It is true that Jesus as an eternal high priest "after the order of Melchizedek" (Hebrews 5:6; 7:15) was preparing to offer up himself as a sacrifice for the people; but he also carried out the prophet's role to the very end.

The same basic concern for the obedient and faithful life is found in the story of Job. It might be imagined that its only concern would be the problem of suffering, but right in the middle of all its questions about suffering we find in this book one of the loftiest descriptions of the ethical life to be found anywhere in the entire Bible. The thirty-first chapter of Job is a magnificent description of what takes place in a person's life when he applies the principles of the

Ten Commandments to everyday situations. A closer look at the Book of Job also seems to indicate that Job is replying to the charges of his "friend" Eliphaz as they are recorded in chapter twenty-two. When we place the statements of Eliphaz and Job side-by-side, we find that we have almost a straight dialog between the two men; and in this dialog they are reflecting some of the fundamental teachings of the law of God.

You Shall Have No Other Gods Before Me

When we look at this dialog, however, we should not be examining it as spectators who are merely interested in deciding which side scores the most points. When he hears the law of God, the believing child of God is called upon to apply it to himself. We look at the mirror of the law in order to see what we are really like in the sight of God. Therefore we are not just overhearing someone's speech; we are hearing God speaking to us. We are not looking at the morality of someone else; we are looking into a mirror which reveals our own true selves.

One of the first accusations which Eliphaz had hurled at Job would fit under the first of the Ten Commandments: "You shall have no other gods before me." When he makes this charge, he uses language that has a familiar ring for our own society. "Throw away your gold; dump your finest gold in the dry stream bed. Let Almighty God be your gold and let him be silver piled high for you" (22:24-25). Job replies, "I have never trusted in riches, or taken pride in my wealth" (31:24-25). Nor has he indulged in the false worship of the sun or the moon (31:26-28).

The mirror can be held up right here. Money is the great god of our times. The acquisition of wealth and the accumulation of earthly goods has become so much a part of our way of life that we take it for granted. When we say, "Now you're hitting him where it hurts!" we most often mean, "Now you're hitting him in the pocketbook." We may not worship the sun or the moon, but no one dare ignore the admonition of the Apostle Paul: "Put to death . . . covetousness, which is idolatry" (Colossians 3:5). Yes, hold up the mirror of the law and let it lead you to an awareness of the truth uttered by Job: "God knows everything I do; he sees every step I take" (31:4).

Love Your Neighbor as Yourself

Conversation about whether you trust in your riches or whether you trust in God can easily become idle speculation, but not an honest assessment of how you use your riches as an expression of obedience to the second table of the law: "You shall love your neighbor as yourself." The largest portion of the dialog between Eliphaz and Job focuses on the treatment of the helpless and disadvantaged, always one of the prime concerns of the Old Testament when it speaks of the ethical life. Eliphaz charges that Job has taken advantage of the poor, ignored the weary and the hungry, and exploited those who could not defend themselves, especially widows and orphans.

Job's defense is a classic exposition of what the Old

Testament understands man's responsibility toward man. As far as the poor are concerned, Job answers, "When I found someone in need, too poor to buy clothes, I would give him clothing made of wool that had come from my own flock of sheep" (31:19-20). He never restricted himself to who should be the object of his loving concern: "All the men who work for me know that I have always welcomed strangers. I have welcomed travelers into my home, and never let them sleep in the streets" (31:31-32). What of the fatherless? "I have never refused to help the poor, never let widows live in despair, or let orphans go hungry while I ate. All my life I have taken care of them" (31:16-18). What others would call shrewd business deals are rejected and denied by Job: "If I have stolen the land I farm and taken it from its rightful owners . . . then instead of wheat and barley may weeds and thistles grow" (31:38-40).

In these words the mirror of God's law is being held up before all of us. It is a mirror Jesus has polished to a higher degree of intensity through the teachings he delivered during those last days in the Temple. It is the theme picked up by the Apostle James in his general epistle when he writes, "Religion that is pure and undefiled before God and the Father is this: to visit orphans and widows in their affliction, and to keep oneself unstained from the world" (James 1:27).

Perhaps we would prefer to lay down such a mirror when it comes to our behavior towards our neighbor, but we cannot. Perhaps we would like to mumble something about how terribly busy our own lives are, or try to escape with a hesitant admission that perhaps we have become a *little* indifferent, but the law of God says, "No, you can't put me down. I will not be lightly dismissed. I am the mirror which tells you of your sin before God."

The Sins of Immorality and Adultery

Eliphaz also makes some caustic observations about Job having chosen to walk in the path of evil which was characteristic of evil men before they were destroyed in the flood. It is about those men that the Book of Genesis comments that the "Lord saw that the wickedness of man was great in the earth, and that every imagination of the thoughts of his heart was only evil continually" (6:5). Perhaps Job is thinking about Eliphaz's insinuation when he becomes very specific in speaking about one area of life where the imaginations of man are very evil, for he begins to speak about his own standards of sexual behavior. Concerning the imaginings of the heart he says, "I have made a solemn promise never to look at a girl with lust" (31:1). He knows that sexual sin originates in the mind and that it is seen as such by God. He also recognizes the inviolability of the marriage bed: "If I have been attracted to my neighbor's wife, and waited, hidden, outside her door, then let my wife fix another man's food and sleep in another man's bed. Such sin would be wicked and would be punished by death. It would be like a destructive, hellish fire, destroying everything I have" (31:9-12).

Here, too, the mirror is set before our society. There is no blurry film over God's explanations concerning sexual behavior. Lust is sin. It is sin on the part of the one who seeks to inflame and excite his own lust for what is forbidden. It is sin for those who consciously seek to create lust. Adultery is sin. There is no place in God's plan for a society of casual bed-hoppers.

The Law of God Leads Us to Christ

We ought to ask how we should apply this thirty-first chapter of Job to ourselves. Our purpose should not be to determine how much Job can rightfully say about himself. Let him make his own defense. God knows whether it will stand the test. Our calling is to accept it as a part of God's law which shows us that we are sinners before God in his holiness. It should make us long for a Savior. In Galatians chapter three the Apostle Paul describes the law as our "schoolmaster" or "custodian." In his day such a man would lead and guide, perhaps even tutor, a small schoolboy. The law of God carries out such a function as it leads and guides us to the cross of Christ where we can find forgiveness for the sins which have been so clearly mirrored for us. So Luther explains the ultimate purpose of God's law: "The law is our custodian to Christ, that is, in order that after being driven and trained by the Law we may be ready to seek and sigh for Christ, for faith, and for the inheritance. For the Law, as I have said, prepares for grace in that it reveals and increases sin; it humbles the proud so that they long for Christ's help" (*Luther's Works*, American Edition, Vol. 27, p. 279).

God's answer to Job or to anyone who would seek to stand up to God on the basis of their own righteousness is this: "I know you. I know you better than you know yourself. I know fully what you see only dimly in the mirror of the law. But I have had compassion on you. I have sent my Son to be the Christ who would become a sacrifice for your sins. He was 'numbered with the transgressors; yet he bore the sin of many' (Isaiah 53:12). You can become righteous in my sight, not by what you have done, but by your faith in my Son. For his sake I will forgive your sins and remember them no more."

The Christian church, in its ancient wisdom, has set aside certain seasons as periods of self-examination. Lent is one of them. It might seem that in our study of the Book of Job we have aimed to limit ourselves to a study of our attitude toward the problem of suffering alone. But the Book of Job is a part of the Old Testament with its consistent, pervading concern about how a man lives, not only about how he endures pain or faces death. Even this book will not let us think of religion only in terms of how our own personal problems and needs are being met. It will not allow that typical approach in which people ask questions only about how God ought to be serving them but neglect questions about how they ought to be serving God.

Therefore, not out of fear of punishment, not out of hope for reward, but because you have found a Savior of the sinful self revealed in the law of God, embrace this magnificent thirty-first chapter of Job, and study it in your own home as a description of the specifics of the obedient life which is lived for God. If you are asked why you have chosen this way, let your answer be that which the Apostle has given: "The love of Christ controls us" (2 Corinthians 5:14). Ask God now to let that love take control of your life.

6.

If you sin, that does no harm to God. If you do many wrongs, does that affect him? (Job 35:6).

He Risks Everything

A visitor to Gettysburg National Park will eventually find himself standing on the high ground known as Seminary Ridge. As he stands at the base of the Virginia statue, shadowed by the mounted figure of General Robert E. Lee, he will find himself looking across a broad, rolling plain toward Cemetery Ridge where the Union forces were massed.

Heartbreak on High Ground

It was from this point that Lee watched the brigades of Longstreet and Pickett's newly arrived division move forward in awesome attack. He watched the gallant troops almost break the Union lines and then turn back, a shattered remnant. Lee turned to his staff and said quietly, "All this has been my fault." He knew that his dream of a victory in the North was dead forever. He would never be able to forget this day in which the noise of battle was "strange and terrible, a sound that came from thousands of human throats . . . like a vast mournful roar." He said again, "All this has been my fault. No one else is to blame." He would continue to lead with honor and distinction, but on that high ground his heart had been broken.

Nineteen hundred years ago there was another hill on which a heart was broken. On a mound called "the skull" or "Golgotha," Jesus was engaged in his greatest battle and all was apparently lost. As his life slowly slipped away, a great darkness covered the land. It seemed as if all creation had gone into mourning as it witnessed the heartbreak of God. His only Son had been offered, spurned, mocked, and now killed. Isaac Watts caught the significance of those gathering clouds in his verse:

> Well might the sun in darkness hide
> And shut his glories in,
> When God the mighty Maker died
> For man the creature's sin.

Vulnerable for Us

The idea of God risking even a moment of anguish at the hands of man would have been blasphemous, if not totally ludicrous, to a young man who emerges in the later chapters of the Book of Job. His name is Elihu, a youth who has joined the three friends of Job in the effort to reclaim Job from his doubt and despair. Elihu speaks with a young man's fervor as he is caught up in a sense of the majesty of God. "Look at the sky!" he challenges Job. "See how high

He Risks Everything

the clouds are! If you sin, that does no harm to God. If you do many wrongs, does that affect him?" (35:5-6).

Can a man hurt God? Never, Elihu would say. Not God as he describes him in his speech recorded in the thirty-sixth and thirty-seventh chapters of Job. Not God who stirs up terrifying storms, sending lightning across the sky; his voice heard in the roar of the thunder while he brings the efforts of men to a complete standstill (37:1-7). God is mighty. God is remote and beyond the highest heavens. God needs nothing from man. Man can do nothing to God. Above all, God is invulnerable. Any other outlook is inconceivable to Elihu.

Elihu has not penetrated to the depths of God's nature. He is not alone. There are many today for whom God, if he is thought of as existing at all, is remote and unfeeling towards man. They cannot understand the nature of God. Later Old Testament prophets, such as Hosea, would offer a revelation of the heart of God which goes far beyond the thought of Elihu. They were able to perceive God as One who becomes involved with his people, even to the point of heartbreak and loss, and this is the meaning behind Golgotha itself. Much more than martyrdom is involved in the death of Jesus. God is involved, risking heartbreak, risking everything for the sake of man.

"I would think that the evil of the world would break God's heart," a man once said to a Christian leader. "It did," the believer replied. No one can fully comprehend the depth of suffering endured by the Son of God. Yet there is a century-old Sunday school hymn, written first of all for unlettered children of the streets of London, that gives us in language simple and unadorned an insight into the mystery of God at work on that hill called "the Skull":

> There is a green hill far away,
>   Without a city wall,
> Where the dear Lord was crucified,
>   Who died to save us all.
>
> We may not know, we cannot tell
>   What pains he had to bear,
> But we believe it was for us
>   He hung and suffered there.
>   (Cecil Francis Alexander)

The heart of God was not merely broken. If that were so, then our topic would deal only with defeat, tragedy, and the power of evil over the forces of good. No, the heart of God was showing that real power and strength lies in the ultimate act of love: the giving of oneself. God was deliberately laying himself open to the worst that lies within the heart of man, and all for one purpose. The New Testament sums it up in words like these: "While we were still weak, at the right time, Christ died for the ungodly. Why, one will hardly die for a righteous man—though perhaps for a good man one will dare even to die. But God shows his love for us in that while we were yet sinners Christ died for us . . . . For our sake he made him to be sin who knew no sin, so that in him we might become the righteousness of God" (Romans 5:6-8; 2 Corinthians 5:21).

The theology of the Book of Job tells us that we

should bow before the almighty power of God. It is certainly true that we do not know the true God if we seek to deny or minimize his majesty and power. But we truly find him and are found by him when we come to see and to believe that his mightiest act of all occurred when through the death of his Son he blotted out our every transgression and made it possible that we could once again belong to him, now and forever. Jesus Christ had everything, the Apostle writes, "yet for your sake he became poor, so that by his poverty you might become rich" (2 Corinthians 8:9). Christ was in the form of God, Paul tells the Philippians, but he risked all in a great act of emptying himself and becoming a servant "obedient unto death, even death on a cross" (Philippians 2:6-9 RSV). As the Wednesdays of Lent draw us ever closer to Good Friday we see that the greatest glory of God lay in his willingness to endure the heartbreak of that day.

The Risk Inherent in Our Commitment to Christ

God became involved and risked all that he might bring us life. Now he leaves us that same legacy. It is a legacy that goes beyond the mere giving of advice to "sinners" which the friends of Job saw as their main task. It means showing love as God showed it; by giving and by taking up the burdens of the helpless.

David A. MacLennan tells about a woman whom we sometimes describe as the "lady bountiful type." She was visiting a hospital ward where a young girl lay dying of tuberculosis. This girl had spent her life caring for her motherless brothers and sisters. Now it was she who was utterly and completely spent. The good lady, however, was much more interested in investigating the girl's fulfillment of her "religious obligations." The young lass did not even come close to a passing mark. The visitor was shocked and filled with concern. With what excuse would this young thing dare to face almighty God? We are told that she "laid two, transparent, work-stained hands on the coverlet. She lifted to her questioner big, dark, glowing eyes, full of peace. Then she made answer too sublime for comment. Very quietly she whispered, 'I will show him my hands'" (*Joyous Adventure,* New York: Harper and Brothers, 1952, p. 88).

You may have noticed that teen-agers who are "turned on" for the Lord enjoy putting up posters like the one that reads, "If you were arrested for being a Christian, would there be enough evidence to convict you?" Well, what about *our* hands? Do they show, symbolically at least, that we have been willing to take the risk of love for the sake of others? The hands of Jesus did, hands hardened first by a carpenter's daily work, hands placed with great sensitivity on the lips of the dumb, hands naturally assuming the position of prayer, hands firmly grasping the cords with which the money-changers were driven out of his Father's house, hands, at the last, pierced by heavy nails.

You and I can adopt our own brand of religion any time and any way we choose. But if the religion of the cross is the one we choose, then there will be risk, the risk of loss or that one's heart will be broken.

He Risks Everything

Dare we even mention the risk of crucifixion? Our finely appointed ecclesiastical structures hardly seem to be suggesting that kind of risk. Oh, perhaps someone has bravely suggested that there is a risk that the monthly mortgage payments on the new church will be difficult to meet during the "lean summer months." But the thought of being rejected because we took a stand on economic questions or social problems or racial tensions, this is too much to ask.

We may welcome the "fellowship" of the church at a Sunday morning coffee hour, but will we risk entering into the suffering revealed through a chance remark over that cup of coffee? Will we risk an involvement in the life of a brother or sister which may become terribly demanding on time and patience? We may send a food basket to the poor, but would we risk the consequence of inviting the undesirables to break bread at our very own table? Discipleship at the risk of crucifixion? Why, even the possibility of being ostracized because we dare to speak against war stops our tongue. Worst of all, we cringe at the thought of being laughed at because we simply take Jesus far too seriously.

It was the conviction of Job's friend that the upright life lived for God removed risk and uncertainty from life. They were, in fact, selling a false bill of goods. Such promises only end in mass desertion and surrender in the face of adversity. But that does not mean that there is no possibility of a life lived with ardor and confidence. It simply means that the power will come from the experience of God's grace towards us, from the discovery that he took a great risk and suffered searing heartbreak in order to bring us back to himself. Such devotion, born of the grace and mercy of God's risk for him, led the Apostle Paul to face the future with these parting words to the congregation at Ephesus:

> And now, behold, I am going to Jerusalem, bound in the Spirit, not knowing what shall befall me there; except that the Holy Spirit testifies to me in every city that imprisonment and afflictions await me. But I do not account my life of any value nor as precious to myself, if only I may accomplish my course and the ministry which I received from the Lord Jesus, to testify to the gospel of the grace of God (Acts 20:22-24).

Sometimes the church has been guilty of presenting the gospel of Christ as if it were offering, at reduced rates, an eternal fire insurance policy: "Stick with us and you won't get burned!" At its best, however, it always offers the religion of the cross: the cross *for* us, and the cross to be borne *by* us with all its attendant risks. Elihu's opinion to the contrary, God risked terrible hurt on our behalf; and his glory was then revealed in a cross. That is where our glory will be found as well.

7. This mob attacks me head on; they send me running; they prepare their final assault (Job 30:12).

He Bears My Sorrows
(Good Friday)

"Look at them! See how they suffered!" This is what we have been saying about Job and Jesus in this season of Lent. The study of Job has reminded us that men can suffer and suffer terribly. The story of Jesus' passion has reminded us that whatever others have suffered, he has suffered, too. Both of them have taught us that suffering goes beyond the infirmities of the body and includes wounding the mind and the spirit, as well.

Now, on Good Friday, when our awareness of the presence of suffering reaches new depths of sensitivity, we take one more look at these two giants facing one another across the pages of the Bible. In fact, the kinship (and the differences) between Job and Jesus can be fully appreciated only when we permit passages from Job and the Four Gospels to be read side by side. As we do, we find each man helping us to understand the other and the message he brings to us.

To begin, both Job and Jesus were servants of the heavenly Father, and initially they received great honor and praise among men. It was Job who said:

FIRST READER:

> "Those were the days when I was prosperous, when God's friendship protected my home . . . . Everyone who saw me or heard about me had good things to say about what I had done. When the poor cried out, I helped them; I helped orphans who had nowhere to turn . . . . I was like a tree whose roots always have water, and whose branches are wet with dew. Everyone was always praising me, and my strength never failed me" (Job 29:4, 11-12, 19-20).

(These passages may be read by the speaker or, for greater emphasis and contrast, by appointed lay readers.)

SECOND READER:

> "As Jesus rode on, they spread their cloaks on the road. When he came near to Jerusalem, at the place where the road went down the Mount of Olives, the large crowd of his disciples began to

He Bears My Sorrows

thank God and praise him in loud voices for all the great things that they had seen: 'God bless the king who comes in the name of the Lord! Peace in heaven, and glory to God!' " (Luke 19:36-38 TEV).

FIRST READER:

And Job said, "When I gave advice, people were silent and listened carefully to what I said; they had nothing to add when I was through. My words sank in like drops of rain; everyone listened eagerly, the way farmers welcome the spring rains. . . . I led them the way a king leads his troops, and gave them comfort when they were discouraged" (Job 29:21-23, 25).

SECOND READER:

"And Jesus taught in the temple every day. The chief priests, the teachers of the Law, and the leaders of the people wanted to kill him, but they could not find out how to do it, because all the people kept listening to him, not wanting to miss a single word" (Luke 19:47-48 TEV).

First Honored, Then Distressed

But the day came, for Job and for Jesus, when the tide began to turn. Distress entered their hearts, and Job said,

FIRST READER:

> "If my troubles and griefs were weighed on scales, they would weigh more than the sands of the sea" (Job 6:1-3).

SECOND READER:

> Jesus "took with him Peter, and Zebedee's two sons. Grief and anguish came over him, and he said to them, 'The sorrow in my heart is so great that it almost crushes me. Stay here and watch with me'" (Matthew 26:37-38 TEV).

Deserted by Friends

We should not be surprised if the masses and casual acquaintances turn away at the first sign of difficulty. What really hurts is the failure of friends to stand by just when one needs them the most. Here, too, Job and Jesus suffered greatly.

FIRST READER:

> Job said, "In trouble like this I need loyal friends—whether I've forsaken God or not. But you, my

friends, you deceive me like a stream that goes dry when no rain comes. The stream is full of snow and ice, but in the heat they disappear, and the stream bed lies bare and dry. . . . You are like those streams to me; you see my fate and are shocked" (Job 6:14-17, 21).

SECOND READER:

"Then all the disciples left Jesus and ran away. . . . Peter was sitting outside in the courtyard, when one of the High Priest's servant girls came to him and said, 'You, too, were with Jesus of Galilee.' But he denied it in front of them all. 'I don't know what you are talking about,' he answered, and went on out to the entrance of the courtyard. Another servant girl saw him and said to the men there, 'He was with Jesus of Nazareth.' Again Peter denied it, and answered, 'I swear that I don't know that man!' After a little while the men standing there came to Peter, 'Of course you are one of them,' they said. 'After all, the way you speak gives you away!' Then Peter made a vow: 'May God punish me if I am not telling the truth! I do not know that man!' Just then the rooster crowed, and Peter remembered what Jesus had told him, 'Before the rooster crows, you will say three times that you do not know me.' And he broke down and cried" (Matthew 26:56, 69-74; Mark 14:72 TEV).

Judged as Condemned by God

Praise and popularity are not lasting. When men want to find fault and pass judgment, they will find their reasons. So we hear Eliphaz saying to Job:

FIRST READER:

"You discourage people from fearing God; you keep them from praying to him. . . . There is no need for me to condemn you; you are condemned by every word you speak" (Job 15:4, 6).

SECOND READER:

"Again the High Priest spoke to Jesus: 'In the name of the living God, I now put you on oath: tell us if you are the Messiah, the Son of God.' Jesus answered him: 'So you say. But I tell all of you; from this time on you will see the

He Bears My Sorrows

Son of Man sitting at the right hand of the Almighty, and coming on the clouds of heaven!' At this the High Priest tore his clothes and said, 'Blasphemy! We don't need any more witnesses! Right here you have heard his wicked words! What do you think?' They answered, 'He is guilty, and must die'" (Matthew 26:63-66 TEV).

FIRST READER:

Bildad said to Job, "If you are so pure and honest, then God will come and help you and restore your household as your reward" (Job 8:6). And Zophar said, "You claim what you say is true; you claim you are pure in God's sight. How I wish God would answer you back! . . . God is punishing you less than you deserve" (Job 11:4-6).

SECOND READER:

"In the same way the chief priests and the teachers of the Law and the elders made fun of him: 'He saved others but he cannot save himself! . . . He trusts in God and says he is God's Son. Well, then, let us see if God wants to save him now!' " (Matthew 27:41-43).

Dying

Job expected that he would die. Jesus *knew* that he was to die. He saw himself as one who was to give his life "as a ransom for many" (Mark 10:45). The prophecy of Isaiah was known to him: "Surely he has borne our griefs and carried our sorrows; yet we esteemed him stricken, smitten by God and afflicted.... Like a lamb that is led to the slaughter, and like a sheep that before its shearers is dumb, so he opened not his mouth" (Isaiah 53:4, 7). In the experience of both Job and Jesus, not a shred of respect or consideration was offered to them.

FIRST READER:

> Job speaks, "This mob attacks me head-on; they send me running; they prepare their final assault. They cut off my escape and try to destroy me; and there is no one to stop them. They pour through the holes in my defenses, and come crashing down on top of me; I am overcome with terror. My dignity is gone like a puff of wind, and my prosperity like a cloud" (Job 30:12-15).

SECOND READER:

> "Then Pilate's soldiers took Jesus into the governor's palace, and

He Bears My Sorrows

the whole company gathered around him. They stripped off his clothes and put a scarlet robe on him. Then they made a crown out of thorny branches and placed it on his head, and put a stick in his right hand; then they knelt before him and made fun of him, 'Long live the King of the Jews!' they said. They spat on him, and took the stick and hit him over the head" (Matthew 27:27-30 TEV).

FIRST READER:

And Job cried, "Now I am about to die; there is no relief for my suffering. . . . How I wish I knew where to find him, and knew how to go where he is" (Job 30:16; 23:3).

SECOND READER:

"And at about the ninth hour Jesus cried with a loud voice, 'Eli, Eli, la'ma sabach-thani?' that is, 'My God, my God, why hast thou forsaken me?' . . . And Jesus cried again with a loud voice and yielded up his spirit" (Matthew 27:46, 50).

Every form of suffering is pitiable, but there is none like that which is endured when even the face of God seems to be hid, that forsakenness summed up by the Psalmist who says, "My tears have been my food day and night, while men say to me continually, 'Where is your God?'" (Psalm 42:3). Job suffered like that. Jesus suffered even more.

The New Man

They suffered—Job and Jesus, and now they will not permit us to hide from the reality of suffering. Instead, they demand that we learn how to deal with it, whether it has happened to us because we have brought it upon ourselves or for reasons which are a complete mystery to us.

As Job faced such suffering, he wanted to argue about it. He wanted to dispute with God as if he were a prince occupying the same ground as Almighty God himself. We can understand his feelings; but God said to him, "Stand up now like a man and answer the questions I am going to ask" (38:3). God would not ask Job to be less than he was—a man; but neither would he permit him to have delusions of grandeur. God reminded him who wanted to act as if he were a divine prince that he, Job, was a man, just a man. He will say the same to us if we need such a reminder.

Then there was Jesus. As the Son of God he had been told to stand as a man before other men, but for an entirely different reason: not because he deserved no other rank but because it was his Father's will that his Son who was so rich should for our sake become poor. He was to become a second Adam because the first Adam had failed. In speaking of this Divine Son we often say that he was truly man. In saying this we mean more than the mere fact that he was actually a human. We mean that he was a man as man truly ought to be, in full and open communication with the Father, totally committed and obedient to the Father's will. He, the Prince of Life, was to take upon himself the plain cloth of humanity so that we might become princes and princesses in the kingdom the Father has prepared for us. He would die on the cross to overcome the power of death visited on all the descendants of the first Adam. Man would conquer, after all, but the victory would be through that broken and solitary figure to whom Pilate pointed as he cried, "Behold the man!" (John 19:5).

It is true that we still contend with death and suffering, but we engage in this struggle as a new people with the unquenchable hope. This is the great affirmation of the New Testament: "In all these things we are more than conquerors through him who loved us" (Romans 8:37). Neither tribulation, nor distress, nor persecution, nor famine, nor nakedness, nor peril, nor swords shall separate us from that man, that long-awaited second Adam, lifted high upon the cross, who has conquered all our enemies (Romans 8:35-39).

When we look at man, in the generic sense, we see a caricature of what God intended man to be. When we respond to the invitation, "Behold *the* man," we see God's promise of salvation and a new life for every man. There are moments when it is fitting to step back from our talk about what we should be doing and simply consider in holy awe what God has done. Good Friday is one of those times.

> The royal banners forward go;
> The cross shines forth in mystic glow
> Where he in flesh, our flesh was made,
> Our sentence bore, our ransom paid.

It is a time to say to Christ, "O Lord, I shall stand before you as a man. Not in a spirit of arrogance and rebellion, as Job was tempted to do, but as one who knows that you have assumed manhood yourself. You know the burden of my infirmities. You have tasted death itself. Therefore do not forsake your own flesh and blood but deliver me as I call upon you for every need of body and spirit. With faith in you I say, 'My eyes are ever toward the Lord; for he will pluck my feet out of the net'" (Psalm 25:15).

8.
>Then I knew only what others had told me, but now I have seen you with my own eyes (Job 42:5).

He Opens My Eyes
(Easter)

Every festival in the Christian year seems to have its own special characteristics. Christmas is marked by a sense of warmth and stillness born of God's peace. There are soft shadows cast by the cool light of a star. Easter, on the other hand, is filled with brightness and the sound of trumpets. Christmas carries with it a sense of expectation, a typical feeling whenever a child is born. Easter glows with an aura of accomplishment: great things have already happened! A new day has dawned through the triumphant emergence of the Son of God from the grave. Whether the outward circumstances are quite humble or extremely imposing, the banners, the bulletins, the colors, and the songs of Easter are proclaiming everywhere today that all mankind has a share in a great victory.

But what is that to us, unless Easter is in our hearts? What does it matter how brilliantly an Easter service has been developed if one's own soul is dead and empty, and life is seen as nothing but a dead-end street leading to the grave? We raise this question because we know that the mood of the world around us, a mood which is sure to affect us all, is not marked by hope and confidence but by cynicism and anxiety.

Nor is it simply the attitude of the world that causes us our problems. There are many of us who have lost one or more loved ones since Easter was last here. Many have found themselves seated in the ashes and rubble of destroyed hopes and plans. There are many who know firsthand the struggle of a man whose life we have been reviewing in this past Lenten season. His name was Job, a man overwhelmed by economic losses, smitten by multiple deaths in his own family, and given over to excruciating pain in his own physical being. How up-to-date his problems sound! Furthermore, these things were happening to a man who gave every evidence of being a follower of God. The question that therefore arises again and again in the Old Testament book that tells us about the sufferings of Job is one we hear today as well, "How could this have happened to me? Why? Why me?"

The Answers Men Give

When people ask such questions, they usually are ready with their own answers. The answers they give are the very kind one can find in the Book of Job. First of all, God himself can be rejected. Job's wife seems to fall into that group when she sees what is happening to her husband. She advises him to curse God and die. Many people have taken this route. They have decided that what they have been told about trusting in God just does not make sense any more. God is dead, or might as well be. The only meaning to life is that there is no meaning, and one must live on this premise. Although often spoken with great bravado, this response reflects the essential despair and hopelessness which has taken over a great part of the thinking of today's world.

The second response to the hard questions of life, also found in the Book of Job, consists of the easy explanation that whatever has happened is the just reward for how one has lived. It was on this premise that Job's friends found it possible to justify the existing order and the terrible suffering experienced by Job. He must have deserved every bit of it, they reasoned. Surely God is always just. Indirectly such people, and they are with us today, are indulging in a spirit of self-righteousness because they are implying that their own prosperity and good health are the consequences of being more righteous than the person who is experiencing so much trouble.

Many of Jesus' enemies used this line of reasoning as he hung on the cross. They asked, in effect, "If Jesus were truly the Son of God, would not God be rescuing him? He *can't* be what he claims to be or else he would not be suffering as he was." This line of reasoning can make us feel quite comfortable when things are going well for ourselves and badly for others, but how quickly despair can then take over should our own house of cards come tumbling down!

Coming to Terms with God

There is a third direction in which the questioning of the meaning of life can take you. This is the direction that Job ultimately took. It led to a direct confrontation with God, resulting in a genuine experience of faith. Job had many questions, as we do, but there came that moment in life when he spoke the words which should come from the lips of every one here today: "Then I knew only what others had told me, but now I have seen you with my own eyes" (Job 42:5). These words point up one of the greatest issues facing the modern world. When it comes to God, have you only heard from others or have you seen with your own eyes?

There is no evidence in our text that Job saw God literally. God is an invisible spirit. What Job is saying is what you can say: "God has become real to me! I have committed myself to him in a genuine act of faith." This must happen, for one irreversible fact about the human soul is that no one else can believe for you. The church cannot believe for you by its provision of an inspiring "order of service." No one else can provide you with the answers to your heart's deepest questions. There must be that moment when you can say, "Then I knew only what others had told me, but now I have seen you with my own eyes."

Can you say this? I know what it means to ask that question and to give an answer. Real faith involves a genuine struggle. It involves making a real choice instead of drifting along, neither hot nor cold but only lukewarm. Job was greatly tempted to give up on the whole business and ask, "So what? What good will all this talk about devotion to God ever do?" In the end, however, he said, "God, I must begin with you in the middle of my life. All else is second to the fact that you are God. You are the Creator. I am the creature." It is with this type of decision that faith begins. The questions, the hard and troubling questions, are still there; but you decide that you will not let them wipe out the revelation of himself which God has offered you.

The Easter Revelation

Now we must go beyond the experience of Job into the experience of Easter. God's self-disclosure to Job had to do with his power and majesty as the Creator of all things. The revelation of God heralded by the New Testament is even greater. It proclaims that God can be known to us, not in earthquake and storm, but through his Son, Jesus Christ. In the midst of all the uncertainties of life, there is now one great certainty: God loves you, whoever you are. God has shown the depth of his love by his giving of his Son for you, whatever you have done. The greatest act of God lies not in the creation of the universe, but in the giving and then the raising of his Son as the Savior of a fallen, sinful world.

Through the great Easter event of Christ's resurrection from the dead there has now occurred a reversal of certainties. At one time the only certainty was that man had failed God and, because of his rebellion, deserved God's judgment. That was the over-riding thought of the disciples in the very first days which followed the crucifixion. As they sat with their heads bowed in shame, they not only asked why this had happened to Jesus but wondered what would now happen to them. They had failed their Lord. They had ignored the law of love. They had been unfaithful. They had fled from the field of battle when he had needed them the most. They had been puffed up with pride in themselves, and now they were paying for it. Yes, from the beginning the moral failure of man has been one of the certainties of life; and death as the consequence of sin has been just as sure, while the question of a future life, a life blessed by God, has been one of man's great uncertainties.

Now all these things have been turned around. Easter has made sure of that. The risen Christ Jesus is the sign of victory. As the living Lord he has power over death. He is the evidence that God has pardoned our iniquity and the assurance that nothing in life or in death shall separate us from the everlasting love of God.

The Beginning of the End

But again we ask, "What is all this, unless Easter is in our hearts?" In the last book of the Bible the risen Christ declares, "Behold, I stand at the door and knock; if anyone hears my voice and opens the door, I will come in to him and eat with him" (Revelation 3:20). Something great happens on Easter when, through the leap of faith, we respond with our own version of Job's words, "Then I knew only what others had told me, but now I have seen you with my own eyes."

Faith in the risen Christ is the beginning of a new life. Christ is in the now. He is able to touch us now, to heal us now, to give power and blessings now. And yet his presence today is only the beginning of the victory and restoration God has in store for us.

Once again, let us look at the story of Job. After he had taken his own leap of faith, marvellous things began to happen. God restored everything to Job, including such items as 6,000 camels and a brand new family. In fact, everything is restored in double measure!

There are some people who do not like this ending. They wonder if it can be genuine. Apparently they would prefer to see Job remain a heroic but tragic figure who lives out his life apart from any earthly or material blessings. The Bible, such detractors to the contrary, has no difficulty with such an ending. The Bible is very materialistic. It speaks openly and joyfully about the good things of this world God pours down on us. This biblical outlook, in turn, has much to do with the nature of what God says will be the final chapter in our own life. The Bible not only says that Christ has overcome death in a real and physical way through his resurrection; but it promises that we, too, will share in his resurrection. "Beloved," the Apostle John rejoices, "it does not yet appear what we shall be, but we know that when he appears we shall be like him, for we shall see him as he is" (1 John 3:2).

What a promise! None of us can fully comprehend all that lies in store for us, but this we know: we shall be restored to the likeness and image of the Son of God himself! This glorious consummation leads the Apostle Paul to exult: "I consider that the sufferings of this present time are not worth comparing with the glory that is to be revealed to us" (Romans 8:18). All we can see right now, the Apostle admits, is a creation "subjected to futility" and "in bondage to decay" (Romans 8:20, 21); but if someone were to ask, "Doesn't this world look like a wreck to you?" we would reply in the spirit of our Easter-born hope, "Yes, like the wreck of a bursting seed!" This is the point of the First Letter to the Corinthians. Paul speaks of the sprouting of the stalk of golden wheat or some other grain from the heart of a decaying seed (15:37). By the power of God new life will come out of death, and on the Day of the Lord we will be, according to the magnificent language of the Bible, "not unclothed but more fully clothed" (2 Corinthians 5:4). Whatever the glories of the bodily life we now know, what lies ahead is not less but more, a time when we will be arrayed in the dazzling garment of the resurrection.

In the light of this hope we face the questions that arise every day because of suffering and injustice. God restored everything to Job in double measure. In the name of Christ he will restore this creation and all those who belong to him in a manner that defies all human ability to measure. Resting on this promise we can possess the faith that overcomes the world with all its burdens. It is the risen Christ who transforms this Easter celebration into a personal victory, inviting us to share in the joy that has led Job and millions since his time to say, "Then I only knew what others had told me, but now I have seen you with my own eyes."